THE ADVENTURES OF ODYSSEUS

from *The Odyssey* by Homer
retold by Martin Waddell

ODYSSEUS

LOTUS EATERS

SAILORS

CYCLOPS

CIRCE

PENELOPE

CALYPSO

TELEMACHUS

ODYSSEUS AND THE LOTUS EATERS

After the fall of Troy, the Greeks sailed back to Greece in triumph, but when they got there, Odysseus wasn't with them.

He didn't turn up for another ten years.

"Where have you been?" his friends asked. "Your son has been everywhere looking for you, and we thought you were dead. You're lucky your wife didn't end up marrying someone else."

"I tried to get home as fast as I could," said the cunning Odysseus, and he told them about his adventures.

When Troy fell, the Greeks destroyed the city, killing as many men as they could before they sailed home. Odysseus sailed with them, but his ships were scattered by storms. His men had a terrible time, until at last they came to the island of the Lotus Eaters.

It looked a lovely island. There were fig trees, and blue water rippled up on the beach, gleaming in the sun.

"Holiday time!" decided the sailors. "We've had enough of storms and battles. We're going on shore to rest, and get our strength back."

"Oh no you don't," said Odysseus.

He needed all his men to sail the ships, and he didn't know what they might find on the island.

"We need water for our ships," his sailors reminded Odysseus.

Odysseus couldn't argue with that … but he allowed only three of his best men to go for the water.

The Lotus Eaters were happy, smiling, sleepy-eyed people. They set the three men down beneath a fig tree, and brought them wine and food.

The sailors tasted the food. It was lovely. "What's this made from?" they asked.

"The Lotus plant," replied the Lotus Eaters. "Do have some more."

"Don't mind if we do," said the sailors. "Bother Odysseus and his ships and his battles!" And they lay down feeling sleepy and cumfy inside.

The sailors who had been kept on the ships began to grumble. "They're lazing about having a good time, and we're stuck out here fixing the ships!"

"Do you want to see your wives and your children again?" Odysseus asked them.

"Of course we do," said the sailors.

4

"So do our friends on the beach," said cunning Odysseus. "But something in that food has weakened their brains. If they don't leave here with us, they will never see home again. We have to save them for the sake of *their* wives and *their* children."

He sent a raiding party to the shore, and they dragged their friends back to the ships. The three sailors tried to escape, but they were too sleepy to struggle. "We want to stay here," they told Odysseus.

"Tough," said Odysseus. "We're going home. And we need you to sail these ships."

He tied them up and they all set sail for home.

ODYSSEUS AND THE CYCLOPS

Odysseus and the Greek sailors came to an island inhabited by Cyclopes. The Cyclopes weren't a bit like the Lotus Eaters. They were huge giants with one eye each, in the centre of their foreheads. They spent their time looking after very big sheep … when they weren't killing people, and eating them that is.

"We've got to land. We need food and water again," the sailors told Odysseus. "The Cyclopes are probably a *little* bigger than we are, and uglier because of the one eye. But we're Greeks! You're not telling us you're afraid of a few one-eyed shepherds, are you?"

"I'll go in with one ship *only*," Odysseus decided, "and we won't attack them unless we have to. We'll bring them a cask of wine as a gift, and try being friendly instead."

"Friendly, *at first*," thought the sailors, who were always ready for a fight.

The sailors landed on the island, but didn't see anyone. They came to a place where the hillsides were honeycombed with large caves, and they went into one. It was neatly laid out and filled with lambs and baby goats in pens. There were lots of cheeses, and pails and bowls of milk, all very large.

"See?" said the sailors. "Shepherds. Maybe one-eyed and a bit big … but they know how to look after their sheep and their goats."

Then a Cyclops arrived, driving a flock of enormous sheep into the cave.

He was huge, and horrible-looking, with a great bulbous eye sticking out of his forehead. Once inside the cave, he rolled a huge boulder over the entrance.

"He's too B-I-G for us!" thought the sailors trying to hide … but it was no use. The Cyclops' huge eye had already spotted them.

"Supper!" thought the Cyclops.

He picked up the two fattest and juicest-looking sailors, bashed their brains out against the wall of the cave, and ate them, crunching up their bones. Then he licked his fingers clean of all the sticky blood and scraps of flesh, and lay down to sleep off his supper.

"Kill him now when he's sleeping!" the sailors told Odysseus. They'd forgotten all about being Greek warriors taking on one-eyed shepherds, now they'd seen the size of the Cyclops.

"*Great idea*," said Odysseus. "If I kill him who is going to roll back the big stone at the mouth of the cave? We'd be trapped in here with his body, and some other Cyclops would turn up and make minced-Greek of us."

"You're our hero," the sailors insisted. "Do something!"

"I need to think first," said Odysseus, and he lay and thought all night, before he came up with a plan.

Next morning, the Cyclops ate two more sailors for breakfast, picked the scraps of sailor out of his teeth with a well-nibbled thigh bone, and set off with his enormous sheep, leaving the Greeks trapped in the cave … and Odysseus got busy.

He took a tree trunk that the Cyclops used as a staff.

"Sharpen one end," he told his men. "Then season it in the fire, so it won't break when I use it."

"What for?" asked the sailors.

"Wait and see," said Odysseus.

The Cyclops came back that evening, and ate two more sailors for his supper.

Odysseus came towards him, holding out the cask of wine. "You'll like this," he told the Cyclops. "It will go down well after all the sailors you've been eating."

The Cyclops drank the wine. It was *good* wine.

"What's your name?" he asked, wiping his lips.

"Nobody," said Odysseus, carefully.

"Well, *Nobody* … as a reward for this wine, I'll save eating you until after I've eaten all the others," the Cyclops said with a horrible grin. "Isn't that nice of me?"

Then he went to sleep.

Odysseus and four of his men pushed the tree trunk into the fire and kept it there until it was red hot. Then they thrust it into the Cyclops' one eye.

The Cyclops howled and sobbed with pain and anger. He rose and stumbled round his cave to find his attackers and tear them apart, but he was blind now, so he couldn't see them.

His horrible screams alerted the other Cyclopes, who were sleeping in their caves nearby.

"Who hurt you?" they called to him.

"Nobody! Nobody!" he shouted to them.

"That's all right then," the monsters outside decided. "If nobody did it, it must be the will of the gods."

They yawned and stretched and turned round and went back to bed.

They were an unsympathetic and hard-hearted lot … just like the Cyclops himself.

The Cyclops was left inside his cave, playing Blindman's Buff with the sailors … being torn to pieces and eaten was the prize for anyone who got caught, and the sailors didn't enjoy it. They hid among the giant sheep, so the Cyclops couldn't find them.

In the end the game stopped.

The Cyclops rolled the big stone from the mouth of the cave, and called his flock of sheep out.

He felt the back of each sheep as it passed to make sure that the frightened sailors didn't creep out with the sheep.

"Now he's taken the sheep away, we won't be able to hide amongst them. When that horrible Cyclops comes back he will eat us."

"Don't worry" said Odysseus. "I've got a plan."

He divided the huge sheep into groups of three, and he made each man hide *under* a number two sheep, the one in the middle.

The Cyclops stroked the back and the sides of each sheep as it passed, but he didn't stroke underneath and so the sailors escaped out of the cave. "We're out!" cried the sailors.

They fled back to their ship, and sailed off to join the rest of Odysseus' fleet.

"No more risks! We want to go home right now," the scared sailors said to Odysseus.

"Me too," sighed Odysseus.

ODYSSEUS AND THE BAG OF FOUL WINDS

The next place the Greek sailors landed was friendly. The king who lived there had been blessed by the gods. He promised Odysseus fair winds that would carry him and his sailors home and gave him a stout leather bag, tied tightly with a string made of silver.

"Don't let this leave your sight for a minute," he told Odysseus. "All the foul winds that blow are held in it. If the winds are let out of the bag, you'll be wrecked and you will never get home."

Odysseus went back on board with the bag but he wouldn't let anyone touch it.

"What's in the bag?" a cheeky sailor asked.

"Just get on with sailing the ship!" growled Odysseus … by this time he was pretty fed up with his sailors.

That started the sailors talking. They wondered why Odysseus kept the bag so close to his side and wouldn't let anyone near it.

"It is treasure he's found on our travels," they decided. "We want our share."

For nine days Odysseus didn't sleep, and the fair winds kept up, taking them home … but at last he was so tired that he slept, with the silver-stringed bag close by his side, where he hoped no one could touch it.

"Now's our chance," said the men, and they crept up to the sleeping Odysseus, and loosened the string round the neck of the bag.

The wind *whooshed* out of the bag blowing the ships off course.

"Where's this wind blowing us to?" wailed the sailors.

"I'll tell you where it's *not* blowing us to!" said the angry Odysseus. "It's not blowing us home."

The foul winds blew them to an island. It had a safe harbour with great cliffs around it that would shield the ships from the sea.

"We've had enough. We're going in!" decided the poor battered sailors, and they went before Odysseus could stop them.

"The foul winds blew us here. I'm not going to land," Odysseus said, and he kept his own ship far off shore, waiting to see what would happen.

The rest of the ships entered the harbour and anchored. The islanders began throwing huge boulders from the cliff tops. The ships were wrecked, and the islanders killed the sailors as they swam towards the shore.

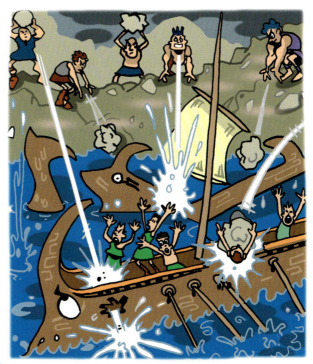

"At least we escaped with our lives, by staying out here," Odysseus told his own crew.

"You've lost all the ships but this one!" moaned the sailors.

"Don't blame me," muttered Odysseus. "I didn't open the bag of foul winds!"

15

ODYSSEUS AND THE PIG SAILORS

"You take a look first," the Greek sailors said to Odysseus, the next time they came to land on an island.

Odysseus climbed a high hill. From the top of the hill he could see a great forest, and the towers of a palace.

"Half of you go through the forest and explore," Odysseus ordered. "The other half stay with me here, near the ship."

That's just like our *hero* Odysseus!" one sailor grumbled. "We take our chances in the forest, and he stays safe with the ship!"

But another one said, "If Odysseus goes first and something happens we've no chance. This way if we're captured or in danger, Odysseus will find some way to save us."

They went on through the forest, towards the great palace, but found themselves surrounded by fierce beasts. There were lions and tigers and wolves were all around them.

"He's done it again! We've been sent to our deaths by Odysseus," they thought, but they couldn't escape … the wolves were in the way. The sailors started shouting and throwing spears at the wolves.

The wolves chased the spears and brought them back to the sailors, like pet dogs playing fetch-the-stick.

Then a lion came up, and licked someone's hand.

One of the tigers rolled over and waited, as though he wanted a sailor to tickle his tummy.

"They're all tame!" gasped the sailors, and they travelled on.

As they drew near to the palace they heard soft music playing, and young maidens singing sweet songs of love.

"Oh boy!" thought the sailors. "This time we're one up on Odysseus. He doesn't know what he's missing!"

A beautiful princess called Circe came to welcome them. She led them into her palace and sat them down to a feast of fine wine and gorgeous food.

"This is the life!" the sailors thought, grabbing as much as they could, stuffing themselves like pigs at a trough.

Circe grinned, as though she'd just thought of a joke. As she passed among them, she touched each of them with a wand, and each one she touched turned, slowly, into a pig.

They were still Greek sailors inside, but they *looked* like pigs, they *walked* like pigs, and (worst of all) they *smelled* like pigs.

They ended up in Circe's pigsty, eating acorns.

All but one, that is. He had been cautious, and held back when the others were feasting. He wasn't turned into a pig and was able to go back and tell Odysseus what had happened.

"Circe must be a great magician," he told Odysseus. "She turns people into animals. There are tame lions and tigers and wolves who must be men she's bewitched, like our sailors."

"I promised we'd rescue them if things went wrong," said Odysseus, and he went off to rescue his men.

A strange boy met him in the forest. He seemed to know who Odysseus was, although they'd never met. He said he'd been sent by the goddess Athena, who took special care of Odysseus.

"This will guard you from Circe's magic!" he said, and he gave Odysseus a sprig of a plant called Moly, which is like the wild garlic that people once used to fight vampires with.

Odysseus came to Circe's palace and she
welcomed him in and gave him good food
and wine, just as she'd done with his men.

Then she tapped him with her wand.

"Pig … go in the sty like the rest!" she said …
But the sprig of Moly stopped her magic from working.

Odysseus raised his sword to cut off her head, but she fell on her
knees and pleaded for mercy.

"Turn my sailors back into men … or else!" said Odysseus.

Circe vowed that she would, and she did … not only that, she
helped the Greeks with the work they had to do on their ships.

"She fancies Odysseus like mad," said the men, but no one dared to say that to Odysseus … Anyway, they were having a good time themselves on the island, with sweet maidens singing of love, and with lots of good wine. There was a shortage of bacon though.

"We're ready to go now," the men told Odysseus, but the beautiful Circe was feeding him grapes and admiring his muscles, so he didn't want to leave.

"Come on!" said the sailors. "We want to go home."

"I *suppose* I want to as well," murmured Odysseus. "That is … I think I do. I'll get ready soon, when I've had my hair cut and I've sharpened my spear. A few days more here … or maybe a week … or ten days … What's your hurry?"

Circe fluttered her eyes, and fed him some more grapes.

"*Odysseus*!" said the men. "Odysseus! We're going home right *now*, this minute."

"Oh all right," sighed Odysseus. "I'm coming."

ODYSSEUS AND THE FOUR DANGERS

The Greeks sailed away from Circe's island.

"Why is Odysseus so worried?" the sailors asked. "We're going home!"

"Circe didn't want him to go, so she has told him stories of all kinds of monsters we're likely to meet on the way," one of them said. "That's my guess anyway."

Then Odysseus started giving them orders.

"Put wax in our ears?" gasped the sailors. "What for?"

"Never you mind," said Odysseus. "And the other bit is … you have to tie me to the mast, and not let me loose till we're past the next island, whatever happens."

"Odysseus has lost his marbles!" the sailors muttered to each other as they tied their hero to the mast.

"Wax! Ears! Now!" commanded Odysseus, and that put an end to the muttering … because they couldn't hear anything.

It was just as well.

Circe had warned Odysseus of the Sirens, sea nymphs whose strange, beautiful singing bewitched sailors so much that they leapt into the sea and drowned themselves.

As the Greeks sailed past the island, the sound of sweet singing came from over the sea … but only Odysseus could hear it. He was bewitched by the sound, and tried to dive into the waves, but the ropes held him fast.

The ship sailed on, until the danger had passed, and his men set him free.

"Satisfied now?" they said to Odysseus, picking the wax from their ears.

"One danger past, three dangers to go!" Odysseus told them. "We have to sail through a narrow channel where there is a great whirlpool, called Charybdis. It sucks the sea in three times a day. If we're caught in that whirlpool … we drown."

"If we see the water suddenly stir, we'll get out of the way," the men decided.

"That's not all," said Odysseus. "A monster called Scylla lives in the rocks close by the channel. She has six heads, and six long necks. She scoops sailors out of their ships, and eats them."

"That's all we needed!" muttered the sailors.

They had to sail on, but they sailed slowly and carefully.

From far away they could hear the great whirlpool roar, and as they drew nearer it seemed to grow worse.

"Concentrate on the sea!" warned Odysseus. "If you see it start to surge …"

Like six lashing whips, out of the rocks came six long slimy green necks. The gruesome fangs of each of Scylla's six heads snapped up a sailor, dragging each one from the ship to her lair in the cliffs.

The sailors wailed and cried for help as they were eaten. There was nothing Odysseus could do.

"Watching the sea, we forgot all about Scylla the monster!" Odysseus groaned, blaming himself.

"You got us past the whirlpool anyway," the sailors reminded him.

"It was my fault those men died," Odysseus said sadly.

But they still had to meet the last danger.

"Next we come to the Isle of the Sun," Odysseus told his men. "We'll only stay for the time that it takes to load water and food on the ship. Don't touch the cattle or we'll be destroyed."

"There's a great herd of cows on the Isle of the Sun," Circe had warned him. "If you land there, you must not touch the cows, or the gods will be angry."

They landed, but the tides and winds turned against them and they were forced to stay. Soon they had eaten all the fruit and vegetables that grew on the island.

"Eat the fish and the birds!" ordered Odysseus. "Don't go near the cows."

"I'm fed up eating bird pie and stewed fish. I really fancy a nice juicy steak," a sailor said, one day when Odysseus was out of the way.

They looked at the cows.

"Steak on legs!" they said to each other.

When Odysseus returned, he found his sailors sprawled on the shore, with a cow roasting on their fire. They were stuffing themselves full of steaks that they had cut from the cow.

He was terrified, because everything else that Circe had told him had come true. It seemed to him that the cow's skin crawled on the ground and the dead cow on the spit moo-ed as it roasted.

"As soon as we put to sea we'll be killed!" moaned Odysseus.

And that's just what happened. There was a great storm and the ship sank. All the steak-eating sailors were drowned … but Odysseus escaped.

Odysseus clung to a raft while the storm lasted, and the waves blew him to the shore of a beautiful island.

He stayed there for a *very* long time, with a lovely sea nymph called Calypso, who looked after him until he got his strength back. Then he sailed on and had more adventures, until he landed alone on the shore near his home.

"Home at last!" sighed Odysseus … but there was one more danger to face.

ODYSSEUS AND THE ARROWS

"Odysseus will come back to us soon," Penelope, Odysseus' wife, had told his son, Telemachus. But Odysseus didn't come. Long years went by, and the boy grew into a man, without ever seeing his father.

"Odysseus must be dead. Whoever marries his beautiful wife will do well," decided the princes from Odysseus' kingdom. They came to the island where Odysseus had lived, hoping to marry her. With only her young son to protect her, Penelope was helpless. The princes settled down to wait in the best rooms in the palace.

"We won't go till you choose one of us," they told Penelope.

She kept putting them off, telling them she had to do first this and then that. They'd just have to wait … and they waited.

"If you don't choose soon you'll run out of money," they told her. "It must be costing you a fortune to feed everybody here."

"I'll choose when I've finished the shroud that I'm making for Telemachus' father," she said. She worked on the cloth every day. But every night, when the princes were asleep, she undid the work that she had done by day.

"You must find your father," Penelope warned her son, "or the princes will force me to marry one of them."

Telemachus went to many places but he couldn't find Odysseus. When he came back to his home island, an old man in rags was waiting for him. "Be careful, my son," warned the old man. "Your mother's suitors are planning to kill you, when you return to the palace."

"Don't 'my son' me!" Telemachus said. "You're not my father!"

"Oh yes I am," said the ragged old beggar, and Odysseus whipped off his disguise. "These men plan to force your mother to take one of them as her husband," he told his son. "I've been with them, but in disguise. Only my dog recognised me. He was very old, but bounded up to me wagging his tail like a puppy. Then he died at my feet. Your mother's guests treated me like a dirty old tramp while they were feasting and drinking at my own table. But we'll settle that score!"

The first
thing Odysseus
and Telemachus
did was to collect
the weapons from
everybody in the palace
and store them in the
armoury.

"Why should we give you our
weapons?" the princes' ringleader
asked Telemachus.

"There's to be an archery trial in the
Great Hall," Telemachus told the ringleader.
"You'll be asked to fire an arrow from my father's
old bow through twelve rings made from axes, set in a straight row.
Whoever succeeds in that task, my mother will marry."

"What's that got to do with taking our weapons?" the
ringleader asked.

"Someone might not agree with my mother's decision,"
Telemachus replied. "We can't have Greek fighting Greek."

"That's what your father said when Helen was choosing her
husband," one of them remembered. "It is almost as if your father
had spoken, not you."

"How *strange*," Telemachus said, hiding a grin.

The next day the princes gathered in the Great Hall. Odysseus' servants barred the doors from the outside, and the contest began. No one had enough strength to even bend Odysseus' great bow …

"Let me try," said the old ragged beggar, and everyone laughed.

"Throw the old fool out on his neck!" growled the ringleader.

"I was *once* a soldier," the old beggar said, quietly. "There's still some strength in these arms." And he added under his breath, *"As you'll soon find out."*

"Let the old beggar have his chance!" sneered the princes.

Odysseus bent the bow effortlessly, and the arrow sped straight through the rings.

"Now for another mark!" said Odysseus, and an arrow sped to the heart of the ringleader, who fell dead on the floor.

That was the signal. The doors of the Great Hall were flung open. Odysseus' servants rushed in, armed to the teeth, and surrounded the princes who had threatened and bullied his wife Penelope. Odysseus threw off his disguise and fitted an arrow to his bowstring.

"Who wants to die first?" Odysseus asked, taking aim.

Blood oozed under the doors of the hall, as the princes were hacked into little bits by Odysseus and his men.

The hero was home from the battles he'd won, and Odysseus' long journey ended as it had begun, with defenceless men being killed in a torrent of anger and bitter revenge.

Odysseus was judged to be a wise man in his time … a brutal time that was kill-or-be-killed. The Greeks called the victories he won their "Glory", though their glory meant slaughter and death.

Perhaps Odysseus was wise enough to know better … but he didn't say *that* to his friends.